TRANCE POETICS

Your Writing Mind

Kristin Prevallet

TrancePoetics: Your Writing Mind
Book two, 2nd edition of the Creative Rewiring Series.
Interim-published by Wide Reality Books.

Book one: *You, Resourceful: Tap Your Inner Resources To Restore Your Mind and Body.*

Book three: *Opening The Field: Language Beyond Language* (Forthcoming, Fall 2013)

Recordings available online at http://www.mindbodystudies.com including guided visualizations read by Kristin Prevallet with hypnotic soundscapes by Ambrose Bye:

Sleep: A 50 minute mp3 designed to lead you into a comfortable sleep.

Automatic Writing (Release Your Writing Mind): a 23 minute mp3 designed to accompany this book.

- This book is dedicated to language
and the field of potential.

Acknowledgements

This book is the convergence of many years of research, conversations, trainings, and experience — both traumatic and restorative. I am grateful to many minds I have never met including H.D., Muriel Rukeyser, Richard Bandler, Clark Coolidge, Milton Erikson, and Charles Olson. And I am grateful to many minds with whom I have had the privilege of sharing airspace who probably have no inkling that their presence in my life is filtered into this book: Mariah Corrigan, Julia Miller, Richard Ryan, Elizabeth Willis, Tonya Foster, Brenda Coultas, Tim (Trace) Peterson, Bob Holman, Lee Ann Brown, Edwin Torres, Robert Kelly, George Quasha, Mei- Mei Berssenbrugge, Toni Simon, Hillary Keel, Bob Holman, Mary Cappello, Laura Hinton, Sarah and Shawn Carson, Cecila Vicuna, Rachel Zucker, Sharon Mesmer, Daria Fain, Robert Kocik, Nick Flynn, Kythe Heller, Brenda Ijima, Anne Waldman, Tony Torn, Brenda Hillman, Ptolemy Tompkins, Abou Farman, Karen Randall, and The Belladonna Collaborative of innovative women writers who graciously accepted me as a member.

I am also grateful to the eclectic breadth of my teachers including Sr. Elaine Prevallet, Melissa Tiers, John Overdurf, Joan Retallack, Bernadette Mayer, Ed Dorn, and Stan Brakhage.

Thank you to Alystyre Julian and to Mariah Corrigan for reading drafts of the manuscript.

TABLE OF CONTENTS

PREFACE

> "Creativity being an ongoing praxis, is a continuous trance, in which one deals with the unification of worlds, rather than fostering inclement fragments. Insights, worlds within worlds, which include not only scintillations of the conscious mind, but more importantly, its ability to both elevate and descend, thereby traversing the triple levels of the mind, the conscious, the supra-conscious, and the sub-conscious minds, creating in the process a concert of worlds."
> - From *My Interior Vitae* by Will Alexander

I met a guy at a party who said, "I'm not interested in talking about trance. I prefer to live in the real world."

And which world is that?

When thought of in the context of the shifty bricolage of various worlds and their corresponding systems (cellular, immune, cognitive, social, political, emotional) that any body is experiencing (enduring) at any given moment, it's hard to imagine any world as "not" real — as not creating and recreating into and around a vast field of possible forms.

"Trance" is one of those slippery words.

Is it a mental event poised between nebulous states of consciousness and hallucination?

Is it the opposite of rational intelligence?

Is it akin to dreams, drugs, and out of body experiences that provoke the "systematic derangement of the senses" prized by Rimbaud?

It can be, certainly.

As revolt, it evokes the unconscious upheaval of the senses and a retreat from "normal" states of consciousness into some nebulous and uncertain terrain where "the unknown" dictates forces unleashed as powers beyond nominal awareness.

But it's so much more than this.

The trance-experiments of the Surrealists found a wide variety of altered waking and near-somnambulistic states of mind in order to generate the artwork or poem. And of course that's very interesting.

But I'd like to expand these ideas into a wider terrain. A trance-state doesn't need to be understood as "altered." Rather, it's a state of absorption that most of us experience in a variety of ways throughout the day as thoughts, and the emotional effects of thinking create vibrations in our bodies causing physical reactions: see something terrifying and panic; think about what is depressing and feel your throat tighten; see someone you love and feel your heart beat a little faster.

So, the trances we fall into through our thoughts can trigger powerful emotional reactions in our bodies (and vice versa). When you think about the effects of stress on your immune system and the effects of relaxation on your heart rate, it's clear that different states of mind affect our bodies at the cellular level, causing biochemical changes.

Milton Erikson, who introduced hypnosis as a process central to therapeutic analysis, defines trance as a "break in conscious and habitual associations so that creative learning can take place. It's a gap in one's habitual pattern of awareness — a critical change in the molecular structure of proteins in the brain associated with learning."

This "gap in one's habitual pattern of awareness" is not separate from all that movement of bodily fluids and plasma, neurotransmitters and hormones, peptides and amino acids. Not to mention the bombardment of waves and particles, neutrinos and atoms, maneuvering as they do into and around information to create the physical world.

What an interesting bundle of contradictions we humans are. We spend so much of our time trying to still what is inevitably flowing, trying to fix in space and time what is inexorably in a constant state of change. As if our bodies and minds obey a different set of rules from the particles colliding, ever moving, within it.

> "Emergent selves are based on processes so shifty, so ungrounded, that we have an apparent paradox between the solidity of what appears to show up and its groundlessness."
> - Francisco Varela, *The Emergent Self*

***

Ezra Pound famously described poetry as the play of phanopoeia, melopoeia, and logopoeia (image, music, and meaning); but there is another "poeia," the one more difficult to analyze because it's simply and so obviously present.

It's the consciousness of the observer (reader) that brings the observed form (poem) into being.

Or, it's the body of the reader and of the writer, either absorbing or repelling, understanding or rejecting, the forms created by other living bodies in a work of art.

Simultaneously, it's what happens when a body experiences the play of image, music, and meaning as these things are present in the forms of the world, and in the forms of art. In other words, the inner process of re-associating and reorganizing, learning or unlearning, based on the information that a body is taking into its molecular design at that particular moment.

It's the movement of the thing. Charles Olson called his process "Composition by Field" and energetically described it as "get on with it, keep moving, keep in, speed, the nerves, their speed, the perceptions, theirs, the acts, the split second acts, the whole business, keep it moving as fast as you can, citizen."

This book isn't a "how to" presentation; nor is it some kind of movement (aside from the movement within the work that's already happening in this field).

It's an effort to acknowledge the psychosomatic information network that connects the bodies of writers and artists to the observing bodies of readers and viewers.

Why?

Well, if only to acknowledge the movable consciousness of bodies and the forms that bodies create. Because the catastrophic future — the one we seem to be headed towards — hasn't happened yet and simultaneously, is happening all the time. And so we keep creating and imagining, not stopping moving, learning, becoming aware of ourselves as alive and therefore participants in the emerging of possible futures.

What Brenda Hillman calls the "tripartite practice" of creation, observation, and activism. In life, politics, love, survival, and change (inside and out).

OUT OF THE BLUE //
INTO THE BODY

If language creates vibrations of thought and keeps thinking alive...

If (as it is known) the space between particles is more intrinsic to matter than whatever its resulting form may be...

If (as it is known) thoughts are conduits of emotion that create vibrations in our bodies causing a physical reaction: think depression and slump, wrinkle, collapse...

If (as it is known) thoughts are powerful emotional triggers, and emotions do affect our bodies at the cellular level causing biochemical changes in the body...

If this much is now understood to be true (which simply means that neuroscience is finally catching up to healing practices people have been using for thousands of years)...

Then language (a conduit to thought) has a frequency and a vibration that can shift our cellular beings...

And if all this is true, then we write a somatic intelligence...

I've studied medicine until I cried
All night. Through certain books, a truth unfolds.
Anatomy and physiology,
The tiny sensing organs of the tongue —
Each nameless cell contributing its needs.
It was fabulous, what the body told.
-from "What the Body Told" by Rafael Campo

***

There is a state of mind, call it confusion. Maybe it feels like a network of knots and brambles in your chest, a feeling of being tangled up in thought patterns that you know are unproductive. Or worse, downright self-deprecating.

I can't do this, I can't see my way clear of this, I'm blocked, I'm down in the dumps. The train of thought is unrelenting.

Until suddenly "out of the blue" a lightning bolt comes down from the sky. Well, not really a lightning bolt. Maybe just a voice that speaks from outside the mind-tangle. Or, like a marigold pushing through the concrete, it's a voice that speaks from inside your mind. And for a change, you listen to it.

Aha!

A profound moment. Your thought pattern is interrupted and you see something that you thought was a knot assume a shape that you recognize as fluid, shifting, and in a state of possibility and change. Like love: a feeling to remind you that you can be *moved*. That no matter how fixed you are in your ideas about things, you are open to interpretation.

Epiphany is a loaded word that carries with it high expectations for the manifestation of deities and face-to-face encounters with gods. Although the likeness of Jesus does occasionally appear in stains, clouds, windows and other objects, an apparition is not required for an epiphany to feel real. But explaining that feeling to someone else requires some mental acrobatics: transforming what is abstract into a story, analogy, or a metaphor.

It came to me out of the blue.

It was like a lightbulb going off in my head.

I woke up on the sunny side of the bed.

It's like I found the last piece of the puzzle and now see the whole picture.

It was a feeling that stopped me in my tracks.

It was like some unseen force that made things start to happen.

A moment when time froze, stood still, or vanished.

It was a profound insight that changed the future.

I experienced a change of heart and a renewed vision of what is possible.

Catharsis or kenosis.

All of a sudden, it became transcendently real.

It's like when something is muddled and then becomes understood.

When something dead is brought back to life, or when a vague idea elicits a moment of clarity.

An unexpected discovery.

And I wasn't even aware that I was thinking of the problem.

The stories and metaphors that we use to describe an epiphany are visual ("I see the whole picture"), kinesthetic ("it stopped me in my tracks") and time-based ("then, suddenly…)

The metaphors we use to communicate the experience of having an epiphany make it sound like a science fiction wormhole that transports your spaceship from where you are right now to somewhere else, in an instant.

And although an epiphany seems to come "like a flash," it probably doesn't actually appear "out of the blue." After all, even the deities of classical mythology and religion did not just appear for no reason — a fate was determined, a course set, the die cast, the star seen in the distant horizon.

So like charting stars, epiphany happens when we have *set the course* for our minds to be predisposed towards thinking an epiphanic thought.

In a 2004 study of neural activity and the "Eureka Effect," scientists concluded that people who experience a sense of insight when posed with a problem had been thinking — at an unconscious level — about the solution prior to solving the problem.

This means that insight happens when there is "recognition of new connections across existing knowledge." A mental territory of "cortical networks" associated with distinct patterns of neural activity, primarily in the brain's Right Hemisphere.

These neural patterns result in the sensation of a flash of insight with no awareness of where (or how) the flash happened. We perceive that the mind plays tricks on us like this, but the trick of epiphany is a mental event caused by the mind's incessant tendency to shift, change, and keep us moving through ever evolving patterns of thought. If it's a trick, it's a good one because it has the effect of reminding us that we're still alive.

LANDSCAPE//MAP

> You get bored with something not when
> you have exhausted the repertoire of its
> behavior but when you have mapped out
> the limits of the space that contains its
> behavior.
> - Denis Hofstader, from *Gödel, Escher,*
> *Bach*

> The distinction between self and not-self
> is made by the decision to claim all that
> the ego likes as 'mine' and to reject all that
> the ego dislikes as 'not mine.' Divided we
> learn where our selves end and the world
> begins. Self-taught, we love what we can
> make our own and hate what remains
> other.
> - Anne Carson, from *Edge*

Our minds create borders around what we
think we know and when we come up
against that edge — when we are challenged
to hear, speak, or see differently — we have
the tendency to recoil or become anxious.

Although brains are malleable, they seem to
have a predilection toward getting into

certain grooves and staying there. The spiked barriers the mind puts up unless a worldview is confirmed: William James calls this "habit."

According to David Eagleman in his book *Incognito*: *The Secret Lives of the Brain*, we think that we see something in the "outside" world (i.e. that robin on the grass outside my window) because the brain works like a video camera, capturing all that we see.

But this couldn't be farther than what actually happens.

What actually happens when we see a robin in the grass is that our brain matches that robin to our expectation of what a robin should be, and how it should behave. This expectation is based on what we already know, and have already seen in the realm of robins. So, as Eagleman writes, "there has to be a match between your expectations and the incoming data for you to 'see' anything."

Which means that if you look at this jellyfish:

You'll strain to see a jellyfish even though your first thought may have been, "that's a creepy claw."

And now if you look at the creature on ice skates...

Your brain will filter, sift, wade, and strive to transform the jellyfish into a much more difficult to grasp fantastical creature (with one big eye).

This is all just to say that we are very good at creating borders around what we think we know; and when we come up against the edge of those borders — when we are challenged to hear, or see differently — we recoil and tune out unless a particular worldview is confirmed. Dogma, the dictum of a penultimate worldview, is the enemy of freedom and yet we conform to what we can and cannot do every day.

And that works in the reverse as well. You could listen to a piece of music you've heard many times before and feel that sense of contentment. But the minute that the notes veer off course and stretch into another configuration of sounds, it's possible you'll feel anxious and want to change the channel.

There's a reason why the 1913 Paris debut of Stravinsky's "Rite of Spring" caused a riot — people's brains were wired to expect a classical symphony, and what they heard sounded like a dissonant attack that assaulted their senses. And in a way, they *were* under attack because the neural networks wired to hear multiple levels of sound at the same time simply weren't there. The collective brains of the audience felt violated and reacted violently. (This isn't an exaggeration. Stravinsky was beaten up and bleeding as he was carried out of the theater.)

But when the composition was played a year later, it was met with enthusiastic approval. Now knowing what to expect, people were able to relax into the experience and it was hailed a masterpiece.

As Eagleman writes, "we believe we're seeing the world just fine until it's called to our attention that we're not." And when what's "not" is called to our attention, watch out.

System overload! Anxiety attack! Revolt!

Or, in time, epiphany.

MOVIE // MIND

There is a scene I just can't get out of my head.

There are images, and this is what I remember (*fade to black*.)

I'll always remember (*fade to black*) the scene.

I'll never forget what happened.

(*Fade to black*) it's ingrained in my mind.

Whenever I close my eyes I see these scenes repeating.

There are images (*fade to black*) and I can see them so clearly it's as if they were real.

Because what happened was internal, beyond words.

Surfacing as images with no frames.

As if these impressions (*fade to black*) are all that survived:

On the slope side of a pasture, wild horses.

Under a tree, a cow.

A woman darts across the burning room to avoid the beams collapsing all around her.

Into the pasture, where the horses quickly disperse.

25

A bomber flies low over a cornfield.

Running through, she has on a dress that matches the flowers.

Picks up a feather and is blown away.

Crushed.

Shattered.

Plummeted.

Flatlined.

She is in smithereens, reduced to shards, smaller than a crumb.

That is what happened.

Scenes, and then (*fade to black*).

Before, and after, in a sequence.

In the clearing, a man and a woman are suddenly present.

After the fade to black, another sequence.

"Nothing," is closure.

Simultaneously, the houses are crumbling.

It's hard to say what happens after that.

***

The desire to surrender to another person's imagination is incredibly satisfying.

"There was a moment in the film when…"

"There was the part of the story where…"

"Listen to this one line…"

Renunciation, submission, take me away.

This is relaxing into vision.

Resting your eyes on colors, vanishing points, memories.

> "That he who looks is always led by the painting to lay down his gaze."
> -Jacques Lacan

A conduit takes you "outside" what you know (supposedly).

A knock on the head from some external force saying "wake up! Pay attention: clarity."

> Suddenly I realize
> That if I stepped out of my body I would break
> Into blossom.
> - James Wright, "A Blessing"

In James Wright's much anthologized poem "A Blessing," an epiphany creates a total bodily transformation. The breaking of his body into blossom breaks the meaning of the poem open in an instant of clarity, the kind that imposes form onto chaos.

It might be said that to have an experience like this is to teleport into privileged airspace. The poet has had an experience and the reader is elevated through the tremors crafted through his command of metaphor.

But as a mental event, the horses do not appear "out of the blue."

The blue is not "out there."

The blue is a convergence of patterns in Wright's brain that cause movements in his mind; and in the mind of the reader.

MIRROR NEURONS

In his pioneering analysis of "mirror neurons" V.S. Ramachandran (neuroscientist and professor and director of the Center for Brain and Cognition at UCSD) made the discovery that when you touch something hot there are motor receptor neurons in your brain that fire off, causing you to pull back your hand. And in basically the same area of the brain there is a subset of neurons, called "mirror neurons" that fire when you see *someone else* touch something hot. And these neurons also fire when you see someone else dive into cool water, or touch another person.

If your mirror neurons "mirror" the actions of other people, this means that your experiences are mirrored in the experiences of what other people are mirroring of other people's experiences — we are wirelessly connected to each others neurons, in other words.

But mirror neurons are not limited to seeing and feeling. Ramachandran posits that they are also involved in understanding other people's feelings (empathy) and that they have played a role in the development of human culture because it is through imitation and emulation that we are able to quickly evolve. In a lecture he said, "we are all merely many reflections in a hall of mirrors of a single cosmic reality."

He goes on to say that in any given moment, the 100 billion neurons in your brain each makes 1000-10,000 contacts with the neurons in other people's brains. Try doing the math — the number of permutations and combinations of brain activity exceeds the number of elementary particles in the universe.

Jack Spicer's metaphor of writing as an antennae open to receiving alien transmissions doesn't seem so far out. Given how we are in a state of perpetual adaption to other brains and their point of view, it's not surprising that we relish moments of epiphany and connection.

In his amazing study *Imitation, Empathy, and Mirror Neurons* Marco Iacoboni describes it like this:

> A classical solution to the problem of other minds is the so-called argument from analogy. The argument from

analogy posits that we first observe certain relations between our mental states and our bodily states and then find an analogy between our body and the body of other people. If there is an analogy between our body and the body of others, there may be also an analogy between our mental states/bodily states relations and those of other people. This way of reasoning about the mental states of other people seems too complex for something we seem to accomplish so naturally, effortlessly, and quickly. Mirror neurons, in contrast, provide a pre-reflective, automatic mechanism of mirroring what is going on in the brain of other people that seems more compatible with our ability to understand others effortlessly and with our tendency to imitate others automatically...

So when you are writing imagine this: your metaphors are what connect your thoughts to the minds of other people. You are the neural network of many brains and language is transmitted through neurons.

And neurons create biochemical changes in the bodies of those minds, automatically.

An Epiphany

Stepping off the train and into the
 fog of the Hudson
            winter darkness has already settled
                    (though it's only 6pm)

        Two boats are anchored
        next to each other,
        bobbing and then pausing
        in time with the current.

                They may as well freeze
                into this movement
                        it seems so easy
        A forceful rise
        a delicate return,
                    between them a
                    movement, that's it.

Out of the blue it occurs to me that
 I'm not thinking about boats
            nor seeing them there
                    on the water —

            And I realize
                in stepping
                 out of my mind
              that the vanishing point of my sight
              is no more, and no less
                    an illusion
                    that presents
                     a shift in the reality
                     I now want there to be.

What does this mean?

Only this:

    To the boats, I abandon

    To the waves, I submit

      I had been thinking,

      "I will not consent."

          And now, I consent:

          That's it.

***

When most people with mirror neurons read or hear a metaphoric story that successfully communicates an epiphany, they experience in their body a feeling of dissipation, like salts in warm water dissolving; or falling back into a feather bed. When this happens at poetry readings you can hear the audible "ahhhh" of bodies exhaling into that moment of internal shifting.

But epiphany's opposite — what might be experienced as a more fragmentary, elliptical transmission of language — also has useful bio-chemical effects.

> "My writing is nothing but a stutter."
> - Rosmarie Waldrop

A stuttered writing (as opposed to a conduit) means that boats bobbing on the river may lead to an inclusive, circulating idea — as opposed to a resolved, satisfied moment.

As Lyn Hejinian writes, this can cause anxiety on the part of the reader who is expecting an epiphany:

> "In the gap between what one wants to say (or what one perceives there is to say) and what one can say (what is sayable), words

provide for a collaboration and a desertion. We delight in our sensuous involvement with the materials of language, we long to join words to the world - to close the gap between ourselves and things - and we suffer from doubt and anxiety because of our inability to do so.

Depending on your pre-conceived understanding of experimental poetry and avant-garde art, you will probably have a radically different experience happening in your body when you read the following poem as compared to "An Epiphany":

"I LIVE IN A BORROWED MULTIPLICITY"
WORD SCULPTING SECTIONS 1-6 OF CLARK COOLIDGE'S "TEN POEMS."

A gust in the atmosphere, cups
clouds, amethyst, buckweed
falls like sun
think the universe goose step back stoop
highway to the moon
blood draws mouth on glass
nervous centipede
ready for the beach

till the ceiling falls

In bed maybe
the smoke
oven, reptiles,
clear light
coffin microbes
walls come in
comets to blame
deep in suffering
mundane shock
correct things
sob story

Tattered tape
try not to slobber
toasties and corn cakes
helmet? hornet's nest?
boats kept snapping
braincase was loose
saw pie melting

Lineaments of fire
sleeping cloth closing in
due to silence
we stayed
quite worn through and bundled

Blow things up
like wacky dingle
dried in telemetry theater
human wails, it's long past time
get the gargoyles to descend
somewhere up near the ceiling
silence brings these things
someone blew it up
or is this copper time

In a hutch
the streets outside
burst
it all slims down
to a point

Golden rockhewn source
your cusp a corpse
will tell you what to do
skin pulls surface moisture
grotesque lasted soul
a mouth pills in short bursts
nothing but strong daylight

Punk trains
fist on the green monkey
latent death
black gleam salt
rosy featured
grass as a pointer
all from one hand

Limited desk
before the metal starts flying
dull, cowards
no way I know to get by
blood in the glass
fixed on futurity

See the bone twist before it falls
you caused all the problems
eyes growing darker
incipient lessons
bark gone scratchy
browbeaten blizzard coming
bullets whiz
brightness whittles

sympathy :
breaks into song.

NEURONS // CONFUSION

I've always believed that art, music, and poetry have the magic ability to "take us out of our minds." Meaning, to defy our expectations and allow us to "see" with a renewed sense of vision; or hear with a renewed sense of listening.

This "renewed sense" doesn't have to mean "pleasant." Often it's in the move into and through the anxiety of uncertainty — "I'm hearing something in a new way, and I don't like it!" — where real learning happens.

Milton Erikson, the father of therapeutic hypnosis, believed that when a person is "stuck" in a problem she is very likely thinking about the problem way too much. All this thinking results in the knotted bramble of neural clusters, all firing to make the problem even bigger.

He believed that if a person allowed even a fraction of a second to knock out these kinds of habitual thoughts with a radically different frame of reference — something that surprised or shocked her so much that her previous patterns of association (the problem) had to leave her body and mind completely — that this moment of "pure awareness" and fascination could result in something new: an opportunity for a shift in perspective.

Neurologically, this is the phenomenological correlate of a critical change in the molecular structure of proteins in the parts of the brain that are associated with learning; the creation of new cell assemblies. Or, to put it simply, the creation of new neural pathways that just might — in the same way that a campfire grows larger with kindling — represent an entirely new way of being, in spite of the problem.

> "Psychological problems develop when people do not permit the naturally changing circumstances of life to interrupt their old and no longer useful patterns of association and experience so that new solutions and attitudes may emerge."
> - Milton Erikson (20)

This movement of mind (and its subsequent re-kindling) involves experiencing change in a way that reconfigures a person's most deeply held beliefs about self and world.

It is this very state of confusion which is probably why you might say that certain books, or pieces of music, "changed your life."

In spite of his reputation for being difficult, Shakespeare has been changing lives since 1603 and a team of researchers from the University of Liverpool wanted to find out why. In an article called "The Shakespeared Brain," they recounted the evidence that reading Shakespeare has a dramatic effect on the human brain (in case you didn't notice).

One of Shakespeare's stylistic feats is his ability to create sentences in which parts of speech are scrambled or used in ways that defy the rules of grammar. For example, "he childed as I fathered" — a line from *King Lear* in which nouns "child, father" act like verbs.

What the researchers realized is that when people read, nouns and verbs are processed in different parts of their brain. So when a person reads sentences that are stylistically difficult, the brain has to fire extra neurons to measure and process the confusion. Those extra neurons result in what they call a "P600 surge."

When our brain encounters difficulty or confusion, it has to work a little harder to fit what is difficult into what we already know. Think of this like a jazz quartet. You've got the bass player keeping the background beat going, while the pianist pushes the melody towards ever more complex vibrations and syncopations.

Even just for a moment. To hear the music of the language instead of the incessant chatter, so often negative, that reverberates through our thoughts. This just might allow knee-jerk reactions such as, "I don't understand this therefore I hate it," to be suspended.

Of course, expecting a work of art or language to provoke a eureka response that escalates into a profound, transcendent, meditative state every single time (and being upset when it doesn't manifest) is the creation of another kind of expectation. But that's ok. After all, the brain functions on expectations. It's being open to creating new ones that becomes a really useful trick for managing moods and getting unstuck from emotional or physical suffering.

And writing into the music of language in brand new ways that may surprise you, and your mirror neurons.

OVER//MIND

> "Form, in music, is expressive —
> expressive to some strange subconscious
> regions of our minds. Music… triggers
> clouds of emotion in our innermost selves.
> In that sense musical meaning is
> dependent on intangible links from the
> symbols to things in the world — those
> "things" in this case being secret software
> structures in our minds."
> - Denis Hofstader, from *Gödel, Escher, Bach*

The "secret software structures in our minds" are the fragments and patterns that we build up and repeat, re-modulating as we take in new information, experiences, actions, and forms. As a mental event that is experienced emotionally, kinesthetically, and in time, an epiphany condenses and synthesizes with the patterns already plotted in our minds.

This happens when conducted via a conduit or constructed via a stutter. What matters are the ever-reaching synapses firing in your mind that strengthen the frequency and intensity.

"That overmind seems like a cap, like water, transparent, fluid yet filled with definite body, contained in a definite space. It is like a closed sea-plant, jelly-fish or anemone. Into that overmind, thoughts pass and are visible like fish swimming under clear water."
- H.D. from *Notes on Thought and Vision*

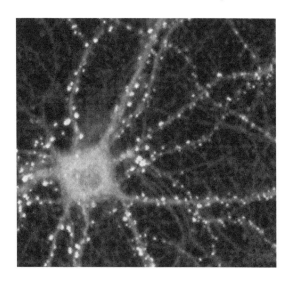

H.D.'s conception of the *overmind* is intensely and personally visual. And yet, her visceral realization that she is capable of transforming thought into a mystical hyper-consciousness is actually confirmed by recent scientific realizations about how the mind works. Her jellyfish tentacles are the synapses that connect all of the patterns and fragments of information that we have accumulated from memories built up as we live our lives. They form a unique underwater-looking system of electric conduits.

And disorientation happens quickly when those synapses become broken.

In the popular press there is one article after another about studies showing us how to avoid mental decline. Drink coffee, do crossword puzzles, avoid excessive daydreaming.

But how about articles on how to communicate with people who have already disappeared into their broken synapses?

The music of broken strings

My grandmother was raised in a St. Louis slum where she met an inspiring man who pulled himself up by his bootstraps into a life of wealth and prosperity. Not wanting to be associated with immigrants, she changed the pronunciation of his last name so it sounded less French. She was always well-dressed, with a tight upper lip, and a severe sense of humor. When she laughed it was always with a glare in her eye.

In old age she was transformed by dementia and for the first few years she was extremely angry and embittered, lashing out at anyone who tried to help her. Then something remarkable happened. Like Oliver Sach's patient Vera B who used language purely associatively and would suddenly break into song, my grandmother — who had shown no interest in music during her life — suddenly started singing. She underwent a total personality change, became uninhibited, smiled all the time, and laughed with total abandon.

As Sachs writes, this transformation is the more positive potential of the return of the repressed:

> The musical or artistic powers that may be released in front temporal dementia or other forms of brain damage do not come out of the blue; they are, one must presume, potentials or propensities that are already present but inhibited — and undeveloped.
> — Oliver Sachs

As her former self my grandmother wouldn't have appreciated that I am a poet and feel at home in free association. But suddenly we were able to communicate in a brand new way. I'm grateful that I had a couple of terrific conversations in the strange musical language she had developed — a language that seemed to bewilder other members of my family and seemed to annoy the nurses.

I remember thinking to myself: "If only they understood poetry and the pleasure of free association — they wouldn't be so afraid."

About a decade later I received a grant to bring poetry to a nontraditional audience, and decided to work with Gary Glazner and the Alzheimer Poetry Project. We walked into a room in a nursing home with twenty 2nd and 3rd stage Alzheimer patients, all in their own worlds. Some were singing, some were talking, some were far, far away.

Gary stood in the middle of the room and started reciting Longfellow's "The Arrow and the Song."

> I shot an arrow into the air,
> It fell to earth, I knew not where;
> For, so swiftly it flew, the sight
> Could not follow it in its flight.

I breathed a song into the air,
It fell to earth, I knew not where;
For who has sight so keen and strong,
That it can follow the flight of song?
Long, long afterward, in an oak
I found the arrow, still unbroke;
And the song, from beginning to end,
I found again in the heart of a friend.

He then started clapping to the rhythm of the poem as he read, and he repeated this over and over until everyone in the room was clapping.

Following his lead, I turned to a random page in the anthology of classic poems and dramatized the cadenced rhythm in the nursery rhyme, "The Owl and the Pussy Cat." (Of course, one spritely gentleman could not refrain from making an innuendo.)

The vibe in the room changed. Suddenly everyone had a poem that they wanted to recite — whether or not they knew all the words wasn't important. They remembered the rhythm of the language and found great pleasure in it. Those who spoke other languages began reciting in their languages. Even a woman who had clearly disappeared into her broken synapses became present on and off throughout the hour. She was there just for a couple seconds at a time, but the nurses said that this was the most response they had seen in her since she had arrived.

Although they have lost many of the threads that interweave their most precious stories and images, those diagnosed with mental lacks of cognition haven't lost the entirety of their memory. They may have difficulty recollecting images and words, but they can respond to the repetitions and rhymes of verses or songs learned at some point in their lives. It must be that music — and the rhythmic structures of poetry — works like a bridge to access aural and kinesthetic memories even if the synapses are broken.

And this opens up channels of

        antennae to

            "non-normal"
            conversation

                (whatever
                that is)

    into the silences &

g
a
p
s.

In "Dementia Blog," the poet Susan Shultz writes of her own creative communication experiences — often painful and testing of the limits of language — with her mother who was in the later stages of dementia.

She writes,

> I have heard those words in those subject/object positions, yes, but what of other sentences, those that refuse closure, open to offer me a middle seat? I will not let go this contested beauty. For each sentence admit the possibility of another, and another. If you are the guilty settler of one sentence, change your noun and verb. The adjectives will follow.
> —Susan Schultz, *Dementia Blog*

And yet for most people, free association is scary and the fear of losing language as a tool for effective communication hinders us from calmly interacting with people who have lost their fluency.

But like Shultz's altering of the rules of grammar in order to communicate with her mother, I wonder if we can all learn to talk with our elderly in their altered cognitive states? (And not fear, ignore, or become aggravated with them.)

William James writes about how music, poetry, and art have the ability to "take us out of our minds." Meaning, outside of the border we put around ourselves. Enabling us to experience a new way of thinking while at the same time preserving the worldview that keeps us safe.

Imagine hearing language that is unhinged from productive communication and understanding that it's not threatening.

Imagine being ok with that uncertainty as it eclipses the person we once knew.

The person whose speech is unrecognizable and yet whose voice still needs to be heard.

Final interview with my Grandmother

Esther: Let me introduce you to my radio. Over here my. What do you call that when. Doll face?

Me: Her hair is so pretty. A coo of plentitude.

(*laughs*)

Esther: And what do you call that? Bears?

Me: I saw one once, across the river.

Esther. (*Eyes big*). Oh my. (*Singing*) "Lions and tigers and bears..."

Me: (*Singing*): For though from out of Time and Place, the flood may bear me far, I hope to see my Pilot face to face, when I have crossed the bar.

Esther: (*Singing and moving her hands up and down as if conducting*) When I have crossed the bar my love when I have crossed the bar...

(*Everyone laughs.*)

ONE FOR THE SPIRITS

On the one hand, automatic writing is an eccentric activity with a strange history. Like the ectoplasm which the Spiritualists believed to be the membrane between the living and the dead, when a person has opened their body to be inhabited by the flow of language, amazing things seem to be able to happen.

Automatic Writing as a tool for divination seems to have been "invented" in the 19th century as news of celebrated mediums such as Mrs. Arthur Conan Doyle (who used automatic writing so that she and Arthur could communicate with their son who had been killed in action in World War I) spread into popular consciousness. During this time the humble Baudin sisters were channeling answers to technical questions relating to physics, of which they seemed to have no prior knowledge; William Yeats and his wife Georgie were contacting spirit guides, which resulted in *A Vision*, a poetic and philosophical theory of history.

It's interesting to think about the popular rise of automatic writing in the dawn of the industrial revolution, which set the stage for the coming 20th century's automaticity of communication through telephone wires and cables.

It's as if the Spiritualists were laying the track for the spread of a communication network that eventually would connect people's minds together in ways that we are, at this moment in time, still experiencing as an unfolding.

It's interesting to think about automatic writing in the context of the progress of communication:

First ancient civilizations built their villages around rivers.

They carved paths through the wilderness that soon other people traversed in covered wagons.

Then railroads were built along those paths.

Then highways, telephone poles, and canals.

Sewage systems and underground pipes to carry water.

Oil pumped from deep under the ground and put into barrels, onto barges, and filtered across the world to fuel "universal human mobility."

Then the internet.

That weaving of wires, cables and central network hubs around the globe is already becoming obsolete.

Because now we're wireless.

And eventually instead of cables, we will traverse the globe through radio waves, or maybe sound waves.

What galaxies will we contact when we are finally telepathic?

***

Like possession, in the 19th century the writing hand seemed to be writing through a voice or personage that came from the "outside." In his cultural study *Modernism, Technology, and the Body* Tim Armstrong charts the shift from the 19th century's conception of automatic writing as a "secondary personality" to the 20th century's more psychological understanding of it as a process that reveals "attention and distraction."

In the 21st century there are still psychic mediums and healers who utilize automatic writing the old fashioned way — as a means to receive information sources that seem to lay "beyond" conscious awareness.

If you are interested in automatic writing as it relates to communication with "secondary personalities," it is instructed that you practice every day for a period of time being open to the moment when you become like a vessel receiving the muse-bathed waters of the Pierian Spring.

Along with the belief that you are contacting external entities, the continued practice of automatic writing just might result in coherent sentences and concepts that are beyond your conscious scope.

But before that happens, you'll probably write a lot of seemingly random words, or indecipherable scribbles. Think of this as the laying down of progressively deeper and more visible tracks through a forest thick with trees and overgrowth. Or, think of it as becoming familiar with a process of being that is at peace with confusion, uncertainty, and doubt. Remembering that learning happens in surprising ways.

Whether you believe that automatic writing is the manifestation of spirits or the more psychological ability of our minds to "disassociate," there is no doubt but that the process is mysterious.

A team of researches from various universities got together to analyze what happens to a medium during an episode of automatic writing. The result is a collaborative study called, "Neuroimaging during Trance State: A Contribution to the Study of Disassociation."

The results of the study reveal what indeed does seem to be a part of the ether into which the unknown blows: automatic writing is not actually writing.

According to the study, in "normal" processes of writing things like memos, scholarly articles, blog posts, etc. the cerebral cortex (the planning area of the brain) is very active, along with several other areas. But in automatic writing, these areas significantly quiet down and yet "the writing that results is highly complex" in terms of ideas, execution, syntax, etc.

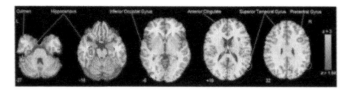

So what is happening?

Clearly "something other than relaxation" is happening that allows the cerebral cortex to shut down. And researchers can't see which area of the brain is firing neural patterns when the person is engaged in automatic writing.

This suggests what appears to be a blatant contradiction: if what we understand as "writing" follows a distinct pattern of activity in the cortex, then is automatic writing "not" writing? And if automatic writing is "not" writing, then what is it?

Here we are, once again, at that time-old question that scientists are determined to prove:

What is the connection between the mysteries of consciousness and the grey, mushy, matter that sits between our ears?

Neuroscience and psychological studies will continue to try and get close to replicating this state of body and mind synthesis on neuro-imaging scanners, neutrino chambers, EKGs, EEGs, and MRIs...let the studies flow on.

With every brain scan and neural feedback loop, the ancient shamanic and spiritual practices that have always indicated the existence of a kind of field are substantiated and brought into a larger awareness.

OPENING THE FIELD

One of the steps that you'll take to induce your automatic writing arm is that you will be asked to disassociate your conscious mind (the part of you that plans, chatters, distracts, and often interrupts) from your unconscious mind (the part of you that loses track of time, gets into a flow zone, and enacts you inner auto-pilot.) You will do this by gradually relaxing the muscles in your body and breathing into any areas of discomfort so that your mind can meander into an unfettered terrain.

Like two trains — one in a tunnel and one above ground — the conscious mind runs on one track and the unconscious mind runs on another. With practice you can quite literally distract the conscious mind so that it can go ahead thinking about one thing, while the unconscious mind sets off on a completely different course: writing, or drawing. You'll be given the suggestion that your writing hand is literally separated from the rest of your body like a prosthetic arm belonging to, and receiving instructions from, a separate consciousness. In this way you will be "disassociating" from your writing arm so that it can move more unconsciously.

In psychological terms, "disassociation" is usually associated with how the protective unconscious mind deals with trauma — by allowing a person to detach from an emotional state, or even from parts of their body. For better or for worse, this can result in a radical form of forgetting — a cover up of painful memories that sometimes can result in an inability to deal with reality in a productive way.

But disassociation is also a normal and a familiar mental activity: it's what happens when we sit down to write and become absorbed by the process; it happens when we daydream and yet still somehow manage to drive from one state into another.

But there is an even larger metaphor that we can use to relay this dissociative ability, one that seems to connect certain "non-behaving" elements of quantum physics with elements of the human body when it is in a healing state. "The field" is a way of fathoming the possibility that our bodies — basically a bundle of singularly designed molecules —

evolve, grow, and exist in relation to a mutable field of energy and information. Our perception of ourselves and the world around us as stable is only because of our inseparability from, and relation to, the field.

As Lynn McTaggert writes, "Matter isn't stable but an essential element in an underlying sea of energy. No matter how slowed down, nothing in the subatomic or atomic universe is ever still."

Think of a rock. And now think about the millions of particles that are zooming around inside of it, giving it shape, mass, and size. If you're up for it, think of the space between all of the particles that are filled with gas, air, or liquid and how that space is what determines the rock's shape and size — it's "porosity" which is defined as "a property that is the ratio of the volume of a rock's empty spaces to its total volume."

And then ask the question: can the rock that I am perceiving as solid really be obeying a different set of rules than the rock whose form is shaped by the space and movement of particles within that space?

Like the rock that sits quietly at the bottom of a river, you can be the body there occupying space with your mass and volume (I'm 5'4, 135lbs). When you are the rock you are conscious and aware that you are a body who is about to sit down and write.

But you can also sit down and write from the perspective of the you who is sitting at that desk because of the energetic movement of particles in space. You can be the agent of interchanging forces, open to receiving from, and giving to, the field. You could open your writing arm into the field of language.

Charles Olson writes of the "Human Universe in which we exist feelingly in the same space and time with the objects of our perception."

In opening your writing arm to the transmission of the flow of language, you are existing feelingly in the same space and time as the field.

And I don't know if when you imagine the field you'll imagine a field of wildflowers, or a field of waves and particles. But you'll know when you're in it, and that's all that matters.

HEART // MIND

Another way of thinking about automatic writing is that when you are able to relax your body and expand your mind, the disassociated hand can write without thinking in the same way that a magician performs a slight of hand *without thinking*; or a tightrope walker walks across the Twin Towers *without thinking*; or a baseball player hits a home run *without thinking*.

You might think that you brain is what will keep you alive in the unlikely event that you encounter a poisonous snake while walking in the tall grass. But you'll be very glad that you're not thinking in that situation, and instead are relying on another organ to step in and push you out of the way: your heart.

A good example is Philippe Petit, the tightrope walker who walked between the Twin Towers before they were destroyed. In an interview he was asked what he was thinking while he was walking across the wire, and he burst out laughing. "You think I was thinking?" he wildly exclaimed. The electromagnetic field of his heart was what was instructing him where to place his feet on the rope. If he had tried to think about it...well, best not to think about that.

According to the researchers at the Institute of HeartMath, your heart has an electro-magnetic field (probably the same field as the one mentioned in the previous chapter) that when measured in an electrocardiogram (ECG) is about 60 times greater in amplitude than your brain waves when recorded in an electroencephalogram (EEG). This means that your entire body is surrounded by a powerful electromagnetic field that can be detected and measured several feet away from your body and between two individuals in close proximity.

So as you begin this process of automatic writing, begin by breathing into your heart simply by taking a deep breath in and counting to six as you raise your shoulders and your chest. As your breath moves up into your upper chest you can know that your heart is feeling that shift, and will eventually respond by slowing down.

Then close your eyes and see if you can hear your heart beating. As you're doing this, imagine that you have an electromagnetic field around your chest and as you fill in the details of that field (what color is it? what quality? what temperature?) you can follow your heart as it leads your brain to a meditative (alpha) brain wave state.

And then write the words of that state as they come to your antennae, now tuned into the field of language.

AUTOMATIC WRITING PRACTICE

[You'll need:

Pen, paper, timer.

To begin, read this chapter through in its entirety. Don't worry about memorizing the steps – rather, integrate whatever you remember about what you have read into 20 minutes of writing practice. If you prefer to listen to a recording, follow the instructions on the copyright page to access it.]

i. Warm up

First we'll begin with a warm-up because with automatic writing it's best to practice not being too attached to the outcome — like any creative state being able to write automatically takes practice and a dose of perseverance.

But because you are right now thinking about yourself automatically writing, you can be sure that the writing has already begun to take shape, in your mind, right now as you think there are words forming in your mind and you can imagine what it will feel like to pick up a pen and begin writing. For now take a moment to do this in your mind's eye knowing that you're starting the process of connecting your hand to your wandering thoughts, and it works just right when you relax any expectations for what will happen and just allow your mind to wander into and among your thoughts, knowing that this is the process of writing the words from your mind to the page, easily flowing, right, like that.

So to warm up, simply put the tip of your pen to the paper and write without lifting it for five minutes, writing non-stop without lifting your pen, eyes open and watching as the ink or graphite rolls or scratches across the page. You can know that getting stuck just means writing down the first word to pop into your mind over and over again, because you're learning how you can get unstuck anytime by writing the same word over and over again until more words come. Because words and thoughts happen in association, one after the other like a chain of bubbles, just like that now pick up your writing instrument and notice yourself writing freely the words, thoughts, associations that come to you, practicing what it means to not be worrying about the outcome.

[Set the timer for *5 minutes of writing*.]

How was that? Take a minute to notice what was happening in your body as you were writing. Did you feel your breathing change, your shoulders relax? Did you hear how quiet it can be in your mind when you're busy doing something else with your thoughts aside from paying attention to them?

And now you know that you can return to writing freely like this anytime you need to slow your thoughts down, breathe, and relax. If you do it every day for a few weeks, you might be surprised what surfaces in the pages you've written — some people discover that they've started a novel or several lines of poetry; others find that they've wandered into memories, or thoughts about things they didn't even know they were thinking...but whatever you wrote, and whatever happens, it's all right — you're doing it perfectly.

And now that you've experienced what it feels like to connect your thoughts and your pen to write freely, without wondering or worrying about the outcome, you're ready for a deeper experience of automatic writing.

ii.

You can begin by finding a comfortable place to sit, where you can write uninterrupted for 20 minutes or so, open to the flow of your thoughts as they intersect with any noises or distractions if they happen to come up. If there is a question you think might benefit from an unconscious response, or a situation in your life that you'd like your unconscious to help you with, you can write it down at the top of your page now.

If you'd like to dedicate your intention during this writing time to a person, dead or alive, who may or may come forward as a guide at some point during your writing process, you can write this person's name at the top of your page knowing that you won't be attached to the outcome, but will be pleased to entertain this person's voice as it comes through your thoughts to your pen. It's important to reiterate to that person your openness to their healing, generative words or lines, those that will inspire you with creative enthusiasm, insight, and focused energy.

Now that you've focused your mind to consciously and unconsciously wander in and around, through and beyond a certain question, or person, or any other intention you might like to bring to your writing time today, you can hold the pen gently in your hand, as if you are preparing to write but are not sure when you will start, noticing perhaps the play of your conscious mind as it acts skeptical, or even resistant, knowing that your unconscious mind is on a different track and is occupied with finding a creative way to communicate through writing, getting words or images across the page in a way that feels comfortable to you.

Knowing that whatever thoughts you may be having are the right thoughts to be having at this moment and at this time, you can be holding that pen and noticing now the fact that it is resting not yet moving, but soon will be writing. And it's useful when opening yourself up to the pen that holds the hand that you can write even more freely if you distance that arm from the rest of your mind and body.

That's right, so the arm that you write with will begin to feel strange, even separate from your body but at the same time quite at ease. You can begin by noticing differences between your two hands. Is one lighter and one heavier? Is one colder and the other warmer? Does one feel a tingle and the other a steadiness?

As you begin to notice the differences between your two hands you can begin to be curious about which one wants to participate in this process here today. Most people have one hand that they prefer to write with, but it's possible that the opposite hand is fidgeting to participate. You can begin noticing little unconscious twitches in one or the other of your hands, and that's a good way to know for certain which hand it is that wants to be the hand that separates from the body and does the writing.

As you become open to this idea of your writing arm disconnecting from your body, feeling at ease knowing how writing happens so naturally, so fluidly, even without being aware that the arm is moving. You can give your writing arm a little lift by consciously raising your hand just a couple inches from the paper, pen in hand.

And you can close your eyes and imagine that the pen in your hand is attached to the string of a balloon, and as you imagine the balloon (I wonder what color it is?) rising so effortlessly into the sky, you can know that your arm can begin to raise as well, making slow, unconscious movements. Just give it a try.

With your arm now attached to the balloon lifting higher into the sky, you can know that this is your dreaming arm. This is the arm that dreams the wild and wonderful dreams that flow from your unconscious mind during the night, whether you remember them or not. And dreams come in so many different forms.

They can come through imagery, symbols, memories, or wonderful movies playing in your mind; they can come as feelings, maybe just a sense of conviction, or determination; calmness or relaxation. They can come in the form of a feeling of being a part of a community of dreamers that have been dreaming long before you arrived, and long after you wake up. Dreams come in the form of sounds, or perhaps just that presence of mind hearing now all that you hadn't been hearing before.

With your dreaming arm in the air take some time to dream — just let your unconscious mind lead you to where you need to go in this moment. And perhaps you will see a symbol, or an animal, or a person; and you'll know it's time to lower your arm.

And as you lower your arm you will be integrating that symbol, animal, or person along with all of the unconscious resources that you have that will help you out with your writing today. And as you feel all of those resources pouring through you from so many parts of your life, into your writing arm, you will know when you can set it once again onto the paper, and begin writing.

You can begin very slowly, pushing it across the page, being aware that you are pushing the pen slowly across the page not sure where it is going; if it is drawing or writing, it doesn't really matter, except that it is moving, that pen pushing across the page, slowly…and as you do this with the pen, another part of you, a more quiet and observant part of you perhaps, can reflect and wonder when to jump in and take over the process, writing unconsciously what you'd like to write, now, keep pushing that pen around and see what happens, see if there's another part of you that might want to add a little loop or an extra squiggle to the end of that line, one part doing one part, another part doing another until all the parts are tops- turvy, and so comfortable knowing that whatever is happening is the right thing to be happening now, open to what happens, and feeling comfortable, that's write.

And when you're writing freely, automatically writing what feels right for you at this moment, enjoying this feeling of your hand moving, just right, in the direction you want to be going, while a part of you can be listening to music, while another part of you imagines a crumpled up piece of paper, just an ordinary piece of paper all crumpled up, and you can imagine while writing that you are smoothing out the folds of the creases in the paper, slowly smoothing them out knowing that whatever you are writing is like the folds of paper, some trace is being smoothed out and that thinking about this while writing you can go even deeper into trance and allow your unconscious to follow creases and folds of its own.

I wonder where it will take you, gradually, and how it feels to be expressing those things, and what conclusions you might be drawing, or writing, knowing certainly there is something to be said about the matter at hand.

Knowing your unconscious mind is making all the meaning you need right now, like gusts in the atmosphere, cups in the clouds, amethyst weed falls like sun, shine un-think, step back, stooping down, moon howl bays, draws cotton, till the sky falls, sleeping, maybe the clock clusters in clear light, dust, walls, deep story hidden, tattered cake, helmet? hornet's nest? boats bobbing, braincase loose, pie melting, beautiful staircase of fire, closing in, stay warm, soaked through and wet bundled, long past time, sky somewhere up near the ceiling, silence brings shadows out, in time hutch, the streets outside, slims down, to a point, golden source, your cusp in thought, compass to where you go now, pulls from surface nourishment, soul, heart, bliss in short bursts, nothing but strong daylight, gleam salt, rosy rain smears windshield, grass as a compass, sound of one hand, daisy, petals flying, getting by with it, down on the glass, reflection fluid, drink, want one, before it falls, deeper eyes growing darker, learning lessons, coming along, you're okay meandering like this, uncertain where you are going knowing you are here, brightness: because writing quiets matter, while your unconscious mind keeps writing, feeling calm, on a matter of course wherever you're going, is right.

[*Set a timer for 20 minutes and integrate whatever you just read into a process. Don't worry about if you're doing it right, or following the exact sequence of instructions.*]

iii.

When you hear the bell or alarm of your timer sound, you can stop writing and find a comfortable place where you can relax. Shake out your writing hand and your dreaming arm so that they will once again feel a part of your body. Your arm feels normal in every way. And in a moment you will be fully awake and once again fully present in the room, knowing that, you'll understand the meaning of what you have written and be able to interpret its meaning, even if it's surprising or not exactly what you had intended or wished for.

Knowing that your unconscious will come forward quickly with some insight or moment of clarity, even if that is feeling ok with what is unintelligible or confusing, that there is clarity in that feeling in your body, relaxing, feeling good, becoming aware of the room, of your body on the chair, rolling your head and shaking your amazingly resourceful dreaming arm, now fully awake.

Interpreting // Uncertainty

When looking back over the writing that may appear to be random, you may get the feeling of being disappointed, as if nothing happened. But just because what happened perhaps defied your expectations doesn't mean that "nothing" happened. Rather, what happened may open up a new pathway to learning something or, could result in a thought/idea you wouldn't have had otherwise. Here are a few suggestions for ways that you can think about your mysterious scrawl:

1) Your Shakespeared Brain

What in your writing seems to be fragmentary mush just might, when you look at it from the perspective of neural surges, be something worth paying attention to. Because when you're writing automatically into language that is coming through your disassociated hand, it makes sense that what will results will themselves be disassociated.

And yet, you can find moments of complex but meaningful examples of syntactical confusion that will cause your neurons to "surge."

You can do this by circling words that "stand out" to you for any reason, and write them on another piece of paper — and then begin playing around with them the way you would if you were molding clay into non-descript shapes.

As you do this notice: perhaps a memory will be sparked. Perhaps a poem will be hidden in the "functional shifts" between parts of speech that at first seemed to lack meaning but which you know now is firing neurons, working into an "emergent consciousness" — meaning that is unhinged from the rules of grammar.

2) Embrace uncertainty

Remembering the importance of having no expectations, slowly look back over what you wrote. If what you did looks more like a drawing either because the handwriting is undecipherable, or because only drawing happened, then take a moment to study the lines, contours, and shapes that you see there. As you either read what you wrote, or study what you drew, highlight any word, phrase, or passage that you find interesting for any reason, keeping in mind that sometimes words and phrases can appear diagonally or between sentences. If what you did looks more like a drawing, you can put a box around any part of the drawing that draws you in for some reason — you might see shapes, or figures appear in different parts of the drawing that you can highlight in some way.

Once you have highlighted interesting or curious parts of what you produced, look at them and free write your first thoughts on the following questions:

What am I seeing in this piece of writing/ drawing? What does it remind me of?

How might what I am seeing reflect my question, or the person who was invoked at the top of the page?

What meaning is being understood through this process?

3) Find the Spin

Like waking up from a dream that you can't remember, just notice how you're feeling in your body right now. How are those areas of your body that usually feel tension? How is your "anxiety hot zone" — that area between your throat and your stomach?

Noticing how you're feeling emotionally, decide if that's a feeling that is useful to you right now. If it is, magnify it and take action.

If it's not, spin it: drop down into the middle of that feeling and notice the direction that it is moving. All feelings move — they are signals carrying chemicals and neuro-transmitters from your brain to your spinal column, to be diffused through your body.

Once you've identified the movement of the thing, reverse the spin of it. Imagine the movement as lifting away from your body and into your cardio-magnetic field. Hold it there for a moment, and then put it back in your body, noticing how effecting the spin affects the outcome.

And then take the first smallest step that you need to take to hold and maintain that better feeling in your body.

Radical Processes

"The complexity of living molecules arises not from the fact that they contain a great variety of different kinds of atoms...but the fact that these four kinds of atoms can be combined in large numbers in many different ways."
— John Gribben

Adrenine, Cytosine, Guanine, Thymine (A C G T): The chemical components that combine to form our DNA create a variety of singular human forms, just as the carbon atom is likewise distinctive for its ability to combine with other carbon atoms into "a molecular strip."

So at the core of our cellular being are permutations — atoms, molecules, particles, DNA, and a whole host of other complex processes that are moving, shifting, and energetically combining to create the form called:

You, Evolving.

And language works in a similar way because letters are just letters until they attract other letters and form a word. Within the alphabet is an expansive variety of possible permutations, and likewise the words that they form are not isolated entities but exist in a series of relationships. "A Word" is a process of expansion and dynamism, into sentences that carry meaning and the potential to open the mind to thought, interpretation, and quite possibly, action.

In the Kabbalist tradition there is a practice called Gematria that reveals the field of dynamic language potential. The practice involves calculating the numerical value of each letter in the Hebrew alphabet so that every word in the Torah is understood both mathematically and linguistically. As Marc Alain Ouaknin explains it in his book *The Kabbala*, "A word is a letter-by-letter construct based on various successive stages, each which has a meaning. Reading involves seeing the word and the world not as they are but in their various constituent parts...."

This means that there is the potential for infinite plays on both the letters and their numerical value that makes it possible to produce an infinite number of interpretations and new perspectives.

Obviously, Gematria is quite complex and as one of the oral laws passed down to the Jewish people from Moses on Mount Sinai, the practice is sacred.

But like many sacred practices, what is revealed is a process of understanding that is so fundamental to "the Human Universe" that it seems important to fold it into this book.

> "A word enters into a dynamic that makes it tend towards infinity."
> - Marc Alain Ouaknin

> "All matter in the universe is connected by waves and spread out through time and space and carried on to infinity, tying one part of the universe to every other part."
> - Lynn McTaggert

> "The inner structure of language recapitulates the inner structure of the world. The poem is a product of vector forces being brought into phase with one another."
> - Charles Olson

PRACTICE RADICAL PROCESS

This exercise comes from Richard Chess, amazing teacher and author of *Third Temple*. Chess explains that although the poetic form of the Acrostic is not a part of Gematria, it's a simple way to experience the meditative intensity of the process.

Take one line from a poem (or a title) that means something to you and rewrite it on a piece of paper.

Take a moment to reflect on how/why this poem is so important to you.

As if you are forming anagrams, take each letter and use it to create a new word.

Put all of these new words in a list in the same order.

Following the order of the list, find a "form" for the words by putting words together that seem to "make sense" (noting that "make sense" could mean that the words sound good together, in a musical sense.) Use space between the words to get the meaning across, and use whatever punctuation you wish.

For example:

The body is the great poem (Wallace Stevens)

Then
He
Erased:

Beautiful -
Odiforous -
Dance -
Yes.

Isabope:
Singular.

Theory?
Haphazard,
Energetic.

Gollum:
Rabblerousing
Element.
Ants,
Tactic.

Plausibility?
Opens
Enough
Meaning.

If meaning is important, it is perhaps along these lines:

First imagine a book.

Then look at how the letters erase themselves one by one, leaving behind three words and no punctuation:

Beautiful

                odiferous

        dance

Then comes the inevitable question: Is there any connection between the remaining three words?

Yes.

Think isotopes.

Think of singular moments in time.

Think in terms of space and the theory of interconnectedness.

It's alright if it feels haphazard, random.

Because of all the filling in, it feels energetic.

Like raising a Gollum to be a rabblerousing element: sun, wind, fire.

> Like following a line through the sand (tactic of ants).

What is plausible about this?

Only that it opens enough meaning for there to be a notion.

***

If you take some time to play with the permutations of words in this way, you might notice that you've fallen into the kind of trance which unlocks a process in which you can be highly absorbed. You might find that it's perfectly relaxing to simply allow it to unfold, with no concern about the outcome. After all, the poem that results may not be what you consider to be a poem at all. You'll be between categories.

But how does it feel in your body to break your habitual understanding of "how a poem should behave" and become absorbed by the act of moving letters around to reveal the internal movement of the alphabet?

Like automatic writing, this is a meditative practice that leads a writer to the heart of the energy that resides within the letters and, perhaps, transmits that energy to the reader. (Especially if the reader is willing to enter into the energetic play of language in order to make his or her own meaning out of it.)

As Janet Zweig writes in her 1996 essay, "Ars Combinatoria: Mystical Systems, Procedural Art, and the Computer," "Finding meaning in new combinations and permuting letters and numbers leads to mystical experiences born out of the meditative activity."

So if you're one of those people who never quite understood how to meditate (because that instruction about "quieting the mind" just never made any sense to you), how is it now knowing that you can pick up a pen, play with the permutations of language, and quite possibly achieve that much sought after feeling of reflective calm?

WORD-VIEW

Although meditative states are certainly worth-while to achieve in the midst of the chaos of daily life, falling into the trance of permutations and procedure has other benefits as well.

The rogue physicist David Bohm believes that the subject-verb-object structure of language carries with it a world view that is then imposed into our speech.

I Am Depressed

is a sentence that attempts to convey a deeply painful internal state of being. And yet, the sentence carries with it a sense of authority, and worse, identity. It is a statement of closed potential that probably is not helpful to the person who is juggling a number of memories, actions, non-actions, events, and/or human exchanges — not to mention the biochemical reactions and inflammations that are being triggered by the immune system — all at the same time. Categorizing oneself in singular terms is rarely a way to begin the process of feeling better.

In NLP (Neuro-linguistic Programming), the therapeutic name for the tendency towards this kind of self-categorization is "Nominalization." It refers to our tendency (at least in English) to turn states of being into nouns, which we then fixate on as defining our state of being.

To get out of this loop, "De-nominalize Yourself" by playing around with the language that you're using to fix your state.

Turn a noun into a gerund, for example:

What's Depressing?

And then start dealing with the list of contributing factors as energetic entities in need of permutation — and action.

To Bohm, recreating a sentence like this by messing with its syntax as if it were an energy, allows a person to *move their own* energy into a more expansive awareness.

Am Depressed I Am De-Pressed I Depressed Am I Am Pressed (de.)

By taking such a sentence and running it through the "N+7" procedure invented by the Oulipo, a literary movement founded on inventing procedures to generate texts based on mathematical formulas.

To perform N+7 you take a sentence, look up each word in the dictionary, and then count down 7 words. You replace the original words with the new words so that I Am Depressed becomes:

Ibid **A**mateur **D**eputy

And clearly the sentence has changed its energy and has lost its limited definition.

Given the enormous industry that is built around anti-depressants, this might seem to be almost insultingly trite as a therapeutic intervention. And I'm not suggesting that it's some kind of magic trick.

And yet, Harry Matthews, one of the most prolific founders of Oulipo, articulates something profoundly instructive in an interview with Lytle Shaw:

> "I'd like to say at the beginning that the approach that I found in Raymond Roussel — getting to material though arbitrary, game-like procedures — was primarily a way that allowed me to get myself out of the place where I was stuck — feeling and thinking certain ways about the world, confronted with the huge difficulty of working directly from that into the production of the text. The

playful procedures gave me something completely different to do and moved me onto another terrain from which I could come back to the material, whatever that might be. I also found very early on that using such procedures allowed me to be much less censorious of myself, of my own experience, because the work of the super-ego, the work of the critical consciousness, shifted from worrying…to solving the problems of the procedures."

What Matthews is describing here — finding that his world-view changed when he shifted his focus from writing "about" his thoughts/feelings to solving "playful procedures" is a way of thinking about the more therapeutic effects of trance when understood in the context of what happens when you disassociate from whatever problems/urgencies you have for just enough time to be able to relax into a completely different field of awareness.

Because it's interesting to see what happens when you then return to those thoughts that had been so pressing (de-pressing), only to find that you've come up with a way of dealing, or taking action in relation to them.

"Exist feelingly in the objects of your perception," as Olson said.

Play. If only to give your mind a break from its habituated patterns of deprecating self-talk, which often have the tendency to run amok into confusion and doubt.

At the core of most sacred texts is the notion of shifting your thoughts from repeating the same stories over and over again that got you stuck in the first place; opening into the field of forms, forces, and dynamics that do make up your experience at this moment.

Just noticing this will change the neurons in your brain.

How's that for an epiphany?

FORM // MEANING

We exist in the perpetual and ever changing soup of chaos, impermanence, and uncertainty, paced towards that supreme quietness: death.

But we also exist in perpetual and ever-changing moments into which we can experience rare moments of clarity, coherence, flow, action, and comfort.

And although in the "feeling" moment when one or the other of these states is magnified — for better or for worse — it can seem as if that state is the sum total of our existence.

There are several photographs taken in the moments preceding the collapse of the Twin Towers in lower Manhattan by people who snapped a picture of the tsunami of grey smoke and debris as it rolled down the street, gathering all that had been taken for granted (cars, street signs, shop windows, people walking).

What is captured in these photographs is the point in space and time in which the colossal wave of debris intersected with all that had been there before. So in the background is a wave of towering grey smoke rolling down the street; in the foreground is the street looking normal — except for the people, running.

I think that these photographs are no different from living every day on a planet in crisis on which there is the simultaneity of chaos and order, destruction and creation, action and circumstance in almost every corner of the globe.

There is the reality of social and political forces that do wreck havoc on people's lives. The global economic collapse continues to uproot hundreds of thousands of people from the lives they had planned. Environmental changes have altered ecosystems and temperatures so that super storms are most likely the new normal.

But this doesn't mean it's the end, or that humans are powerless.

As Brenda Hillman, poet, teacher, and former hypnotherapist writes in her essay "The Trance Method":

> When I started doing hypnotherapy it was in response to a suffering I thought was quite particular to my own life, but

also with the interest in expanding perceptions. What I found was that, the deeper I went into particular images, the more my experience seemed collective....

The hope that an individual human life might create things of beauty for the culture, or that we will revise institutions — families, schools, systems of law and government — to modify the suffering for human and inhuman species — that hope is constant and sustains energy for the individual search, and even for the general or metaphysical search. That search could be as purely anarchic as art itself: a human life might be conscious in its own terms and might have an utterly strange field of meaning, so that a wise but wild mental act might add to the store of available reality.

To attend to social ills meant attending to the unconscious in images and sense perceptions outside the rational. The benefits of such a search would radiate outward into social and political realms. Stepping into the large pool of images in which the particular imagination interacts unpredictably with a collective experience is mostly what interests me about the trance method.

It's quieter down here. Not a world, only a sense. "Not" where you had not been a moment ago. Rather, inside, soul-reflective-insight-place, dissipated confusion of sight, anxiety, spirit. We can go this way, or another: both lead to the same field, the same open space where not trying, "not" going anywhere but here, it's the earth that moves as it spins around the sun, rock of oil, rock of molten, metallic, core, upon which you are still, very still. But for the wars, and all the rage; but for the words and everything they can't say (and yet stir a universe of neurons, all the same.)

Here seems like a good place to begin.

WORKS CITED:

Alexander, Will. "My Interior Vita." *Callaloo*, V22, No.2, 1999.

Armstrong, Tim. *Modernism, Technology, and the Body.*Cambridge University Press, 1998.

Bohm, David. *Wholeness and the Implicate Order*. Routledge, 1980.

Davis, Philip. *The Shakespeared Brain*. http://moreintelligentlife.com/story/the-shakespeared-brain

Jung-Beeman, Mark *et al*. *Neural Activity When People Solve Verbal Problems with Insight*. PLoS Biology 2(4): http://*e97.doi:10.1371/journal.pbio.0020097*

Carson, Anne. *Eros the Bittersweet*, Princeton UP, 2000.

Eagleman, David. *Incognito: The Secret Lives of the Brain*. Vintage, 2012.

Hejinian, Lyn. *The Language of Inquiry*. University of California Press, 2000.

Erikson, Milton and Rossi, Ernest. *Hypnotherapy: An Exploratory Casebook*. Irvington Publishers 1979.

Glazner, Gary. The Alzheimer Poetry Project.

H.D. Notes on Thought and Vision. City Lights, 2001.

Hillman, Brenda. "A Trance Method." http://www.drunkenboat.com/db16/brenda-hillman

Hofstader, Dennis. *Gödel, Escher, Bach: An Eternal Golden Braid*. Basic Books, 1999.

Iacoboni, Marco. "Imitation, Empathy,and Mirror Neurons." *Annual Review of Psychology*, Fall 2008. http://www.nmr.mgh.harvard.edu/~bradd/library/iacoboni_annurevpsychol_2009.pdf

James, William. "Habit" from *The Principles of Psychology*.

Lacan, Jacques. *The Four Fundamental Concepts of Psycho-Analysis*. Karnac Books, 2004.

Matthews, Harry. Interview with Lytle Shaw. *Chicago Review*, v. 43, 1997.

McTaggart, Lynn. *The Field: The Quest for the Secret Force of the Universe*. Harper Perennial, 2008.

Olson, Charles. *Collected Prose*. University of California Press, 1997.

Peres, Julio Fernando *et al.* "Neuroimaging During Trance State: A Contribution to the Study of Disassociation."
http://www.plosone.org/article/info%3Adoi%2F1
0.1371%2Fjournal.pone.0049360

Perkins, David. *The Eureka Effect: The Art and Logic of Breakthrough Thinking*. W.W. Norton, 2001.

Ramachandran, VS. "The neurons that shaped civilization."TEDIndia, 2009.
http://www.ted.com/talks/vs_ramachandran_the_n
eurons_that_shaped_civilization.html

Sachs, Oliver. *The Man Who Mistook His Wife for a Hat*, 1985.

Schultz, Susan. Dimentia Blog. Singing Horse Press, 2008.

Ouaknin, Marc-Alain. *Mysteries of the Kabala*. Abbeville Press, 2000.

Varella, Francisco. "The Emergent Self."
http://www.edge.org/3rd_culture/varela/varela_in
dex.html

Waldrop, Rosmarie: "By The Waters of Babylon," *Conjunctions*, 2006.

Write, James. "A Blessing."
http://www.poetryfoundation.org/poem/175780

Zweig, Janet. "Ars Combinatoria: Mystical Systems, Procedural Art." Art Journal, Fall 1997.
http://www.janetzweig.com/zweig.ars-combinatoria.pdf

FOR FURTHER READING:

Bandler, Richard and John Grinder. *Frogs Into Princes: Neuro-Linguistic Programming*. Real People Press, 1979.

Berssenbrugge, Mei-Mei. *I Love Artists: New and Collected Poems.*

Carson, Shawn, Sarah Carson, and Jess Marion. *All Puffed Out: A Quit-smoking Workshop for Hypnotists and Change Workers.*

Coolidge, Clark. *A Book Beginning What and Ending Away*. Fence Books, 2013.

Duncan, Robert. "Often I Am Permitted to Return to a Meadow" from *The Opening of the Field*. New Directions, 1960.

Glissant, Eduard. *A Poetics of Relation*. University of Michigan Press.

Lipton, Bruce. *The Biology of Belief*. Hay House, 2008.

Notely, Alice. *Grave of Light: New and Selected Poems*. Wesleyan University Press, 2008.

Perlmutter, David and Villoldo, Alberto. *Power Up Your Brain: The Neuroscience of Enlightenment*. Hay House, 2011.

Pinker, Stephen. *The Stuff of Thought: Language as a Window into Human Nature*. Penguin Books, 2007.

Sarno, John. *The Mindbody Prescription: Healing the Body, Healing the Pain*. Warner Books, 1998.

Scalapino, Leslie. *How Phenomenon Appear To Unfold*. Litmus Press, 2011.

Siegel, Dan. *Mindsight: The New Science of Personal Transformation*. Bantam Books, 2010.

Stevens, Wallace. "The Motive for Metaphor" from *The Palm at the End of the Mind*. Vintage Books, 1971.

Vicuna, Cecila. *Spit Temple*. (Edited and Translated by Rosa Alcalá. Ugly Duckling Press, 2012.

Waldman, Anne. *Structure of the World Compared to a Bubble*. Penguin, 2006.

Yeats, William. *A Vision*. Kessinger Publishing, 2003.

Kristin Prevallet is a consulting hypnotist certified through the National Guild of Hypnotists and an Integral Life Coach certified through the International Association of Counselors and Therapists. She is trained in a number of additional healing modalities including energy psychology, iridology, and frequency healing. She holds a M.A. in Humanities through the University of Buffalo and has received residencies and awards from the New York Foundation for the Arts, Naropa University, the Poetry Society of America, George Mason University, and Spalding University. She currently directs the Center for Mindbody Studies where she leads workshops and works with private clients. Her writings on poetics and consciousness have appeared in a variety of publications including *Spoon River Review, The Chicago Review, Fourth Genre,* and *Reality Sandwich*; she is the author of four books including *You, Resourceful: Return To Who You Want To Be, I, Afterlife: Essay in Mourning Time* and most recently, *Everywhere Here and in Brooklyn: A Four Quartets.*

Follow her blog: http://www.trancepoetics.com

Correspond: kristin@mindbodystudies.com